Don't Get Married Get A Five-Year Contract

By

Lori Jae Ricci

First Edition: March 2013

ISBN-10: 148393263X
ISBN-13: 978-1483932627

DEDICATION

I would like to dedicate this book to all the people who have given me their enormous support for my strong beliefs in seeing marriage, as we know it, dissolved. I would especially like to thank my editor, Amy Serafin, for having continued patience and dedication in getting this book published. Without her, my ability to get focused would have been impossible. And a big Thank You to my children for believing in me and supporting my endeavors. May we continue to embrace our diversity in thought. Thank you to all.

Lori Jae

I Consider Myself Just: "One of the Perfect Imperfect Pieces of the Perfect Puzzle"

Part One

I wonder if other writers get fat? I am sitting here with my voluptuous breasts lying down instead of being perky, my tummy full of chocolate, my coffee in reach and my thighs looking huge. Hopefully when I get my little book done, I will have gotten myself back into a "shape" that conforms to better health. See, I have just started writing and immediately began to move away from my subject. When this delirium of thought takes place, I may go off on a little side trip with my thoughts but will eventually get back to the content that I am actually writing about...no promises though. This is exactly why I want to write this book. It is about promises, vows, oaths and commitments that will be broken.

First let me introduce myself, I am a beautiful goddess that loves men. I have been in the business of sticking my nose into other people's business for over 30 years, first as a hair stylist and then as an Intuitive/Psychic Reader. I have raised two children that are sane and still have their sense of humor. I was married twice and since divorced. This book is not about divorce. This book is not about trashing men or women. This book is about concepts that will hopefully have the reader asking themselves serious questions about what is a marriage. To let you know the direction that I will be going with this book, let me sum it up--I believe strongly:

The idea of marriage is not a natural state for human beings and it has become a component of society from roots that no longer bring the results that was once expected by a less sophisticated population. Marriage has evolved from a way to create peace among Nations to a personal, emotional experience designed to bring two people together through commitments, vows, promises and oaths to stay together for the rest of their lives. Marriage has become a way of life that needs to be dissected and looked at from a non-emotional point of view. Monogamy, which has become a large component of marriage, will have special attention. I feel monogamy is not a natural state of being, for either sex. It is my belief that monogamy is a choice we make on a moment-to-moment basis. It is not something we should swear to as we may encounter others that excite, tantalize and make our hearts race. After all, we change our minds, our bodies and our lives every moment of everyday.

Therefore, I put forward that marriage and the idea of marriage in this day and age should be replaced with Partnership Contracts. We should have five-year contracts that we sign and by the end of those five years, or whatever amount of time deemed acceptable by both parties, we will be asked to sign another contract. If either party does not re-sign the contract, the contract will become null and void and both parties released from the Partnership according to all the provisions of the aforementioned Agreement.

Now that you know what I am putting forth within the pages of my little book, I hope you stick around to see where I go with this concept. These are just some of my thoughts and I will continue to express my story, my suggestions and my ideas within the pages of this book. If it does anything at all, I hope that it would promote the dissolution of marriage as we know it and bring forth a new perspective in how we approach combining our life with another person's life. And may you stay together for as long as you both may *choose*.

Ah, Love, Fabulous, Infinite Love!

Let's talk about "Love". It is the fabulous feeling that gets us to the place of wanting to combine our lives with another person in the first place. *I love, Love!* Love is wonderful.

I also believe that Love is not an emotion but a "Truth". In other words, LOVE IS. It has and always will be present within the magnificent ability of us, the human beings of the Universe, to be able to partake of this marvelous "Truth" at will.

I define a "Truth" as a specific phenomenon within our reality that encompasses a philosophy, a philosophy that resonates with individuals in a Divine, Cosmic, Spiritual or Physical belief system. It is only a "Truth" for you if you can accept it as such.

We can behold the thought of Love, feel it, and have the warmth, fun and enjoyment of it. We can play with it, we can use it, we can taste it, smell it in the air on the mist of spring. We touch it inside the beauty of all that is and we see it in the colors of this magnificent earth. Love churns within the turbulent and exciting spiral of experience. Our senses delight in its aura with the utmost purity of being on a plane of existence where we can use our senses to actually become one with this mystery.

Love is still a constant in the worst of times. As we go through our hells such as illnesses, the complexities of family, births, deaths and traumas of all kinds - Love is still present. Love is infinite. Our spirit, which is made up of vibrations and energy is also infinite. Vibrations create the energy that hums through our beings. This connects us to our Known

Universe along with other Dimensions and Parallel Universes. We have difficulty grasping, with our limited mind/body potential, all which is infinite - ALL THAT IS. Some people may want to relate to it through the terms: God, Universal Power, Great Spirit or Force and/or the Matrix. These constants of change, vibration and energy, are present *within* Love; Love being part of the ether where we bring conscious awareness to reality. We form those realities out of the ether. Therefore, *We* are the creators. *We* are the creators of all that is within our reality. Our realities have no boundaries. So we have infinite potential. Our realities are created for experience and ignited by change. Love, too, is ever present.

Love just exists. Everything in the Known Universe just exists. However, within that universe there are explosions, creations, destruction, reconstruction, beginnings, endings, all which equate to Change. Love is infinite. It has no beginning and no end. We, along with everything else, are small universes contained within the confines of the human body. Love is like the container and emotions and experiences are the "soup" within.

Things that happen within the universe happen to us as well. As in the universe around us, our explosions could be known in the emotional body as anger and hate, in the physical realm as aneurisms and strokes. We create through our thought processes and by having children. Destruction takes place in the form of accidents and illnesses while reconstructions take place with the healing of our minds and bodies. Beginnings happen with birth and endings happen with death. While these cosmic and earthly happenings spiral on, they will coalesce within a Universal Vibration. This Vibration creates Energy within an Infinite Truth, one of those Truths being Love.

We deconstruct as our inner universe helps to create our experiences in life such as illness and trauma. It takes us to the extreme of mental and physical "bottoming out", and then begins the reconstruction of our being, which is healing. Even though again and again stars explode, it is through this destruction that a new planet, moon, or star will be born from the "dust" of the explosion. A new "us" will emerge as that which does not work for us anymore shall be shed, creating ourselves anew - a fantastic ability!

We need illnesses so we can have people triumph through recovery, while stretching the minds of the researchers more and more and new discoveries come into the world. Every time there is a new medical breakthrough, there is also a "new" disease that appears. For every hell there is a heaven, for every war there is a hero, for every death there is a birth and for every blue sky there is a storm.

Love with another person takes on its own dimension. It makes us happy, silly, passionate, romantic, fluid, soft and carefree. When you blend it with lust, you have a combination that can only take us to what is heaven on earth.

Hell is also made up of love - Tough Love. Sometimes we make our own hell on earth through not accepting the Love that resides within our beings. Being honest to others and with ourselves is processing self-love and could be a way to bring about experiences with less drama. Remember the duality of being. We have contentment, we have trauma, we have fun, and we have drama. Sometimes drama is fun; and sometimes trauma can bring about an internal awakening. All exists within our lives with the one constant in life being change.

Love and Lust together are the most potent of inner drives. That combination has brought nations, women and men of all backgrounds, either to ruin or challenge us to find an inner grandeur. One way or another, we can destroy when we want to possess and jealousy becomes all-consuming; we take down not only ourselves, but as in past history, nations have fallen and peace turned to war because of a jealous, possessive love.

Purity of love or what we like to call "unconditional love" is a goal that we seek. Somewhere between the extremes of ruin and grandeur lies the experience of fantastic physical, emotional love that we express for another. We are bringing to reality that which exists esoterically. In our present physical state, we can partake of the Universal Truth of Love.

I don't believe humans are really able to feel either unconditional love or true bliss, let alone sustain these states of being. We can strive for them philosophically. I doubt it exists within our natures, as we are only parts of the perfect puzzle, not the perfection. We are not meant to be perfect. If we were, there would be no use for experience or the earth plane.

Even the love of a parent for their child or grandchildren is not unconditional love, but probably the closest we have to that state of being. A parent still has expectations for their child, therefore a child may be judged when a parent's expectations go unfulfilled, conflict arises and parents and children may emotionally hurt each other. So even in what society considers one of the closest of loves, there is not unconditional love. Even though unconditional love is something that is carried within us, it is a part of the perfection. We get close to it, but as imperfect beings in an imperfect world, we can only seek perfection, not obtain it. That is why we drive ourselves crazy trying to be perfect.

Perfection is a state of being that does not really exist on the earth plane. Perfection is the whole of infinity and what it might encompass. We are perfect imperfection by ourselves. Nothing is, can or should be perfect. The ideal of *perfection* is philosophically driven. I delve further on the subject of Perfectionism in the other book I am currently writing, "Let's Think, Shall We?" Yes, I blatantly mentioned my other book (in progress).

Ah, true bliss this Love. Many consider some Love, "true bliss". However, can we really feel true bliss? I feel that through the sexual orgasm, we are as close as we can get to true bliss. That moment of climax has to be nearest to what a human can feel as bliss. However, I believe that true bliss is the sensation that we feel as we relieve ourselves of our bodies at the time of death - the all encompassing emotion and physical release. That is why the climax, the orgasm, the total release of our mind along with the physical is actually the closest we come to death without dying. Therefore, it is the closest we can come to true bliss while still in the physical being.

And most of us crave it. The sexual drive is extremely powerful as it brings together the physical and emotional. A sexual orgasm allows us a peek at death without us having to leave our existence in this dimension. We are such fantastic creatures, as we can create a form that may develop into a life while at the same time experiencing a part of our future death - that being the true duality of life meeting death. It is a unity that exemplifies the continuous spiral of the human spirit, an infinite human spirit.

As a "Truth", Love also exists within us. We talk about learning to love ourselves, however that love already exists. Our journey is to learn to accept it. This book takes us on a different journey. It is one that talks to us in relation to knowing that Love can and always will be there for us. Love allows us to enjoy certain energies that come to us in the form of another man or woman. The journey I want to take us on is one that will take us away from centuries of manmade rules about our conduct, and takes us to an experience for our spirits to feast upon. A journey that believes no man or woman should be held back from the experience of some of the aspects that make us crave each other.

We don't tire of Love. We tire of each other. We tire of the loss of passion and the loss of romance. We desire the feeling in the pit of our stomachs when we know we will be kissed or kissing someone new. Our senses come alive again. We walk brisker, we feel better and we care. This could all stay alive within us. It is my belief, that if someone is with you because they truly feel that you are "the one" for them, and not because of a vow or commitment hanging over their head, then it can become a lifetime of joy for both. We need to keep our relationships fresh. If you ignore your partners' needs then your partner may leave the contract.

When we take the vow, the oath, the commitment stating, "...until death do us part", we should be overwhelmed. After all, it means forever and eternally, always with just one person unless one of you die. No wonder we get tired and it should also scare you silly. Not all of us are able to keep such a commitment. Knowing ourselves and being honest with that inner part of us first, is the basis to an honest arrangement between two adults. Maybe we would be better at this whole thing if we just didn't have to swear to it. That is the concept that I would like to get across, honesty within one's self.

Society along with religious beliefs have a way of telling us what and how we "should" do things. Then you have within society many different opinions on how to do all these things such as, "how many" children we should have, "how to" get married, and when it fails - "how to" get divorced. The statement that makes me cringe is when people say, "When the sex stops, don't fret, at least you will be married to your best friend." NO THANK YOU! I have friends and enjoy our friendships, but when it comes to my partner, I want the man that lights my fire. If he is also my best friend, then it is a bonus that I would appreciate greatly. Yes, Love, ah Love, how did we get so far away from the Truth of Love?

Marriage, UGH, Marriage

Marriage. What is marriage? Well, I went to several sources for a proper definition and in all honesty, I loved what Wikipedia had to say.

Marriage (or wedlock) is a social union or legal contract between people that creates kinship. It is an institution in which interpersonal relationships, usually intimate and sexual, are acknowledged in a variety of ways, depending on the culture or subculture in which it is found. Marriage can be recognized by a state, an organization, a religious authority, a tribal group or local community. It is often viewed as a contract.

Notice that in the definition of marriage, the term

contract and legal is used. Marriage is a CONTRACT and it IS legal and binding and that is why you need a lawyer or a judge to dissolve your marriage.

All I am asking when reading this book, is that you look at commitment and marriage from a different point of view. If you should get married you are entering into a legal contract. However, you are doing so without any legal clarification on the terms of your partnership. If you entered into any business partnership, you would make damn sure that you had legal clarification on what was expected out of the partnership and how to dissolve said partnership. The marriage contract is the only partnership contract where people are not negotiating terms or planning the dissolution of the relationship. People say that it is "unromantic". No, it is stupid.

What I am proposing is not that radical, but it will be to certain religious communities. All I am strongly suggesting is that rather than enter a contract for life (until death do you part), you break down your Partnership Contract into small bits. If you spend the rest of your lives together that is your CHOICE. A contract helps keep you protected in cases of unseen circumstances. You can still love each other for life; you just continue to re-up your contract.

Why do we feel the need to get married? Simply, our

need to marry comes from deep roots in tradition, history and religion. This tradition of marriage has gone on for so long, that it has become an "acquired need" and is not necessarily an emotional one. I was reading Edvard Westermarck's, *History of Human Marriage, Volume 1* and I about jumped out of my chair with glee when I read this: "As for the origin of the institution of marriage, I consider it probable that it has developed out of a primeval habit." That is exactly how I feel. We get married out of habit.

Alright, so who the heck is Edvard Westermark? He has been described as "the first sociobiologist". He wrote three very large volumes on the history of human marriage, so you could call him an expert on the subject.

When you visit the history of man, you will find that ancient people lived in tribes and hunted for food. Ancient people typically lived in a "communal marriage", indicating by this word that all the men and women in the community were regarded equally as husbands and wives to one another. Typically, the women in the tribe had intercourse with multiple partners and paternity of a child was not an issue. The continuation of the tribe was all that mattered and the entire tribe provided for and raised the children.

As time went on, some tribes began settling down by

becoming farmers and started to cultivate the land and grow crops to sustain the community. That is basically when the transition from nomadic tribes to civilization occurred. With glorious civilization came rulers and kings, markets, property, economics, etc. That is when the paternity of a child became important, not just among rulers, but among the common farmer as well. There emerged a new desire among people to keep and pass down "property/land" to their heirs and NOT the community.

The earliest record of marriage contracts dates back as far as the time of the ancient Egyptians – the greatest farmers of them all. It is from them that most of current wedding and marriage traditions originated. Ancient Egyptians actually negotiated marriage contracts and not just in terms of the dowry, but the main purpose of the contract was to establish the rights of both parties to protect their possessions and privileges during the marriage and after, should they divorce. Marriages were recorded by a scribe and typically followed by a celebration consisting of a banquet with guests, singing and dancing. Divorce was easily initiated as the terms of the divorce were already decided before the marriage, and typically the husband was obligated to provide financial support to his ex-wife after the marriage dissolved. By the way, the government took no interest in marriages or divorces; they deemed them a private matter between couples.

Ancient Greece and Rome continued the marriage tradition that the ancient Egyptians had set forth, but marriage was seen more as a fundamental social institution. Although marriage was important, it was viewed as a practical matter with no romantic significance. Fathers typically arranged marriages for their children and the young couple typically did not meet until the day of the wedding. Unlike in Egypt, [i]women were considered inferior to men and remained confined to the home. Their main function as wives was to produce children and to manage the household while their husbands tended to public affairs. For their erotic needs, men often turned to prostitutes and concubines. As Demosthenes, the Greek orator and statesman explained it: "We have prostitutes for our pleasure, concubines for our health, and wives to bear us lawful offspring."

In ancient Rome, women had few rights as a Roman husband had power over his wife and children, whom he could punish, sell, or even kill as he saw fit. Ancient Israel didn't fair much better, [ii] the status of women was low—they were regarded as the property of their fathers or husbands and could do nothing without their consent. The main purpose of marriage was procreation and the perpetuation of a man's name. Every healthy person was expected to marry. Single men and women were despised and a man could have several wives and concubines.

For the most part, marriage was a personal and civil agreement between parties until the rise of Christianity in Medieval Europe, when the Roman Catholic Church began taking a deeper interest in marriage and created marriage prohibitions. In doing so, the Church greatly strengthened their influence over marriage and required couples to follow religious doctrine in order to marry. As a matter of fact, even today, the Catholic Church still requires Catholics to follow their marriage laws in order for the marriage to be recognized by the Church. Interestingly, European medieval poets and bards that would sing lyrical verses about courtly love, between the 11th and 13th centuries, were the first ones who thought of "courtly love" in the same way we do now. However, throughout most of the Middle Ages and for the greater part of the population, marriage remained a practical, economic affair. Romantic love hardly had any place in it.

During the 16th and 17th century, a debate started on the Church's influence over marriage. The Protestant Reformation Act of the 16th century rejected the prevailing concept of marriage along with many other Catholic doctrines. Even Martin

Luther declared marriage to be "a worldly thing . . . that belongs to the realm of government", and a similar opinion was expressed by Calvin. The English Puritans in the 17th century even passed an Act of Parliament asserting "marriage to be no sacrament" and soon thereafter made marriage purely secular. It was no longer to be performed by a minister, but by a justice of the peace.

Then in the 18th century, England decided that both government and religion should be involved in the marriage process. Lord Hardwicke enacted the *Marriage Act of 1753* requiring that all marrying couples had to purchase a marriage license and that all marriage ceremonies had to be officiated by an Anglican priest in an Anglican Church. The Act did not apply to Jews and Quakers, however, if you were Roman Catholic, Muslim, Hindu or any other religious denomination you had to be married in an Anglican Church in order for your marriage to be recognized by the English government.

It wasn't until 1837, that England started recognizing civil marriages as an alternative to *Marriage Act of 1753* and allowing ministers of other churches to register marriages performed in their church legally through the government.

Since 1837, civil marriages in England and Wales have been recognized as a legal alternative to church marriages under the Marriage Act of 1836. In contemporary English common law, a marriage is a voluntary contract by a man and a woman, in which by agreement they choose to become husband and wife.

In Germany, civil marriages were recognized in 1875. This law permitted a declaration of the marriage before an official clerk of the civil administration, when both spouses affirm their will to marry, to constitute a legally recognized valid and effective marriage, and allowed an optional private clerical marriage ceremony.

With this brief peek at history, you can see how a lot of the marriage ceremonies and traditions came about. Marriage is archaic and rooted in religious tradition and ritual, which doesn't make it appropriate for the NOW! Nor does it make it appropriate for YOU! So   ask yourself, is getting married necessary or are you falling into a learned heritage of traditional rites and ceremonies? Is this where our "need to get married" comes from?

Is Marriage Right for Today?

If you want to get married, have dreamed of getting married, live to get married and all you think about is being married, then you really need to think about this in different terms then some romantic fantasy.

This is for both sexes...because believe it or not, there are a lot of men out there that think that they have to or want to get married. Why do people *think, need and want* to get married?

Do you feel by getting married you are more important in society? Is it that marriage validates your role in society? Are you afraid of bucking the trend and being ostracized from society, your family and/or a religious group?

Remember – marriage is a habit. Do you want to fall into a habit or do you want to make a CHOICE? You are in charge of your life, don't forget that! And keep in mind, sometimes people want you to get married and have children because it validates the choices they have made.

Do we get married to feel we belong in society? We all seem to have the need to belong to something. That is why we congregate in society. It starts with children having cliques and finding the people they want to play with until they change with age. We want to be accepted. We want others to like us. We want to be a part of something small, medium or large. It doesn't matter as long as it is part of our life, society or the world. That seems to be born within our energy.

We can't deny that we all want to belong

somewhere. Even a nonconformist conforms to those who do not conform. So we end up "belonging" somewhere whether we desire it or not. It seems to me that "belonging" is a truth of our nature. Maybe it is because we are all linked together by the matrix; that web of existence which we call the Universe, and maybe that is why we all conform to get married. Marriage is accepted. Therefore we believe marriage is needed, but that is an illusion. Marriage is just filling a need to be accepted, not an honest desire to be introspective and learn about our own psyches. We spend more time getting an education to prepare us for a job, then the amount of time we spend learning about our future spouse or partner.

People will be drawn to marriage until we as a society release our hold on this antiquated ritual. We can make the choice of who we want to be. Both sexes have earned that. No one from family, religion or society should dictate to us whether or not we should work or stay home with the children, how we run our lives or whom we should love. We have veterans and lots of heroes and heroines that have given their lives so that we have the right to choose many things in our lives, so let us not insult them by NOT allowing ourselves CHOICE amongst our freedoms.

I want you, the reader, to think of a new way of joining together those who wish to be together, without anyone demanding unrealistic expectations. That is why I am in favor of abolishing marriage in favor of Partnership Contracts.

It is my belief that on this earth plane, for us to expect either a man or a woman to stay within a marriage and be with the same partner for the "rest of their lives", "for as long as they both shall live" or "until death do us part", is worse than any other vow, oath, commitment or promise that could ever be uttered from either sex at any age or time, let alone making this statement just a few years after puberty.

That is why I find it so difficult to believe that marriage belongs in this day and age.

Marriage In Our Society Today

Society has clearly changed from medieval times. Heck, it has changed since a 100 years ago. In today's Western society, women can now vote, own property, file for divorce, keep their children, they can earn their own income, choose whom they wish to marry and decide when they want to have children (birth control).

Men's roles in society have changed as well. Many men are facing new challenges in their traditional roles, as they are no longer the "rulers" of their castles. Their wives may earn more money than them. Their wives may be more successful in their careers then their husbands, and some men are choosing to stay at home and take care of the offspring.

Strong women can be very sexy, and a man who knows how to use his sensitivity can go a long way with women. What a wonderful, exuberant time we live in to see so many fabulous paths being unraveled before us.

In a world with more and more choices, people are not choosing the typical traditional roles, but are creating new ones. Often making choices that do not include marriage as evident from the dropping marriage statistics. [iii]From 1970 through 2008, the US marriage rate has declined from 76.5 to 37.4 marriages per 1,000 unmarried women. That is a staggering drop. It is also a huge sign that people are no longer looking at marriage in the same light.

However, it should be noted that co-habitation statistics are rising. So although people are not saying "I do", they are still making a commitment to each other without any protection that a Partnership Contract would provide.

Why We Keep Falling Into the Marriage Trap (When It's Clearly Not Working!)

If marriage and our roles in society as men and women have changed from 100 years ago, why do we keep falling into the marriage trap? It's hard not to when society and marketing keep telling people they should. Look all around you and almost everything is about sex, sex, sex and more sex. Well, sex sells doesn't it? Marketing sells the fantasy of romance and love (really lust) and we buy it hook, line and sinker.

Society starts defining our roles the minute we are born. Girls are color coded in pink and boys get blue. Little girls are given baby dolls that eat, poop and spit up, Easy Bake ovens, and a "Bridal Barbie", everything that prepares them for being a wife and a mother. Typically, little girls are not given medical or science kits (although that is changing), tool belts, army men, fire trucks or police cars. Little girls are told to play dress-up, enter beauty pageants (sorry, scholarship programs) and hope to find their "Prince Charming". We take our daughters to movies about princesses who are rescued by a man, a prince, a vampire, an ogre or whatever.

Thank goodness, that in modern society we are encouraging our young women to go to college and seek a profession, however society is still giving young girls conflicting messages. Society tells them to be educated, somewhat independent, self-reliant and yet passive.

Little boys are not encouraged to be fathers or to be husbands, but rather they are encouraged to choose a profession. Boys are given medical and science kits, tool belts and benches, fire trucks, police cars and G.I. Joes, etc. As young boys mature, they still are not pushed to marry as girls are, as boys are encouraged to go "sow their wild oats" allowing them to screw as many girls as they want before they "settle down". While girls are expected to remain virginal until marriage, which brings up the question, whom are these boys screwing if not the virginal girls?

Which brings up one of those comments you hear from people who feel you shouldn't have sex before marriage (or probably a contract too) because they feel if you do have sex ladies, he won't want to marry you. They actually say: "why buy the cow if you can get the milk for free!" Are you kidding me?

Will you please look at that statement! Cow, milk, buy! Is the woman not a person who can have consensual sex simply because she enjoys it? Does she have to bribe a man like he is some dumb fool that cannot live without her "milk"...that statement is so wrong on so many levels, I will let you think about it without further comment.

So back to why we are falling into the marriage trap. Let's look at pop culture shall we. For those of you that watched the Twilight movies or read the books, at any point did you ever see Edward and Bella sit down and talk about what they wanted from their relationship? No! All Bella wanted was to be with Edward, despite her needs, her family, her friends or the danger of turning into a blood sucking creature. All she focused on was her lust and her need to be with this vampire. Maybe romantic in some people's eye, but hardly realistic.

Let's take the most famous classic love story, Romeo and Juliet. Romeo professes his love for Juliet on her balcony, two hours after meeting her and then they get married the next day so that they can have SEX. I get that the play has time constraints, but in reality, this is a LUST story not a LOVE story. They married in a state of haste and in a state of lust. At no point in any of these stories did you see or read any of the characters discussing what they wanted out of their relationship before they married.

Society and marketing give you a romantic fantasy relationship model not a realistic one. The problem is that we model our modern day relationships on these romantic fantasy stories. Let's be real, do you really think Edward and Bella or Romeo and Juliet would still be married today? Society and marketing very rarely give people a relationship model where a couple sits down and discusses the hard and important topics of their relationship such as, what do they want from the relationship, will they be faithful, do they want children and how they will be raised, which family will holidays be spent with, where do they want to live, money and finances, goals as individuals and as a couple, and on and on. These topics are generally avoided because relationships and life are messy, traumatic and sad, but can also be wonderful, organized, spiritually rewarding and sexually charged. But messy doesn't sell, does it?

So with marriage statistics dropping and a divorce rate still hovering around 50%, why are people still getting married? Is it marketing and society? Is it romantic fantasies? Or do we want to be picked? I was reading a brilliant blog from marketing genius, Seth Godin that was entitled "Reject the tyranny of being picked: pick yourself". He was talking about people that are self-publishing their books and posting their own music videos and finding success, but in that article I think he hit on a key component of our culture and our psyche, which is that in some respects as individuals we want validation of our worth. In essence, in much of today's society, marriage still equals worth.

There is a part in Seth's blog that I thought really hit the point home. "It's a cultural instinct to wait to get picked. To seek out the permission and authority that comes from a publisher or talk show host or even a blogger saying, "I pick you." Once you reject that impulse and realize that no one is going to select you—that Prince Charming has chosen another house—then you can actually get to work...No one is going to pick you. Pick yourself."

Yes, he is talking about marketing, but he is also talking about our culture and he hit the nail on the head. As a culture/society we do condition each other to be picked and therefore confirming worthiness. When a woman gets engaged she shows off the ring to everyone. The ring is a symbol that she has been picked. That she is worthy. Have you ever known a woman that was in a long-term relationship and was driven crazy by the fact that her boyfriend hadn't asked her to marry him after so many years? I am sure at some point we have all met this woman. This woman is waiting for her man to tell her she is worthy. That ring, that proposal is what makes her valuable in her eyes.

Men don't feel the pressure to get married as women do, let's be honest ladies, men are not conditioned to get married the same way women are; however, there is a worthy factor associated with marriage for men as well. Ask any man that has proposed to a woman how nervous he was. I have read where many men were terrified during their proposal; the fear of rejection being very real for them and the possibility of humiliation if she didn't say "yes" to his proposal. Did she find him worthy and pick him?

So here we are doing this little dance of validation, waiting to get picked. Truly think about it folks, we are waiting for permission from another person that we are good enough rather than seeking validation from within. This is why people keep falling into the marriage trap. Can you reject this impulse, this conditioning and be honest with each other? Can you tell the person you are in love or lust with all the things as an individual you need in order to have a successful relationship? Are you willing to accept that the other person may not be able to fulfill your needs, wants and desires? And are you willing to walk away from a relationship knowing that you are worthy of receiving those things? And if they can't give them to you, will you find someone else that will? I hope so! I hope you know your worth!

That is why I am for Partnership Contracts and not marriage contracts. Partnership Contracts will force couples to address their individual needs before committing to each other (I don't mean marriage or living together and having kids, etc.). This does not mean they won't contribute to the community that is built within their lives. It means that we (individuals) need to take care of what makes us tick first and then we can contribute to others. For example, before a plane takes off, the flight attendants explain about emergency procedures and advise passengers to "place the air mask over your face FIRST before trying to help anyone else." Why? Because if you are dead from no air, how could you possibly help anyone else. It becomes very clear, very quickly, how we need to prioritize our lives.

Desperation/Desperousity

We often fall into the marriage trap because of our feelings of fear, desperation and neediness. I acknowledge that many of us experience feelings of desperation and neediness, especially when we get to certain ages, and that is why desperation and neediness make us feel we have to get married. My daughter coined the word, "desperousity" -- meaning: A frantic state of mind that leads us into marrying anyone who will ask or consent to marriage. Men and women combined.

I experienced my own feelings of "desperousity" to get married, because it was ingrained within me in my youth having been brought up by Italian parents in a Catholic home. As the baby of three children, I got the least amount of discipline because I learned from seeing my older sister and brother getting "clobbered", that I didn't want to go down that road. Therefore, I kept a great deal within and observed as much as I could. Of course, I did mess up one time by coming home at 2 a.m. and met my father's fist. There was a chipped tooth, my mother yelling at my father and the realization that I did not want to go through that again.

I may not have had a fear of life in general, but with parents from an era of "girls are meant to just get married and have children", I was constantly feeling the pressure that I needed to get married. I was not allowed to go to college as my father felt it was a waste of time and money. He felt a woman just went to college to get married so why not cut out the middle step. I was strongly urged to go to work after high school, make money, find someone and get married. It was very simple in their minds, but not in mine.

Like me, many women in the past felt desperate as family and society judged women who weren't or didn't want to get married. There had to be something wrong with HER, but never HIM. Yes, most of the "hims" of the planet got away from the "having" to get married, but some men found themselves eventually in the position of being asked many of the same questions such as: "What's wrong with you? Why haven't you found someone? Are you EVER going to settle down? Do you live with another man or woman? Do you want to have children? You know there are dating sites? There are plenty of men/women out there and you can't find one?" And the best yet, which all single people ever born despise: "Would you like me to fix you up?"

Men still get away easy in society with not having to be married, as most of society's big pressure falls on the woman. Being a single, independent woman was not acceptable when I was growing up. All I heard was, "you know you aren't getting any younger" and after you had enough Italian women clicking their tongues and shaking their heads at you after making that statement, you found yourself scared, very scared. Of what, I'm not sure, but it had to be bad. Perhaps it was that whatever the elders were clicking their tongues about was and could be very disconcerting. You didn't dare ask what the clicking and head shaking was about as you might then be confronted with the disapproving frown and the raised eyebrow. You were just scared enough by them to think they knew something you didn't, so maybe you should just sit there and be quiet and do as you were told.

Even with all of our advancements, society still feels a married person is better than a single person or perhaps they are more accepted by society. We have to consider radical changes in our attitude towards marriage. As a society, let us condone pure, simple contractual agreements between partners and hopefully stamp out feelings of desperation, as desperation should not haunt us.

Why do we continue to feel that desperation? Because, society and marketing promotes it. Not only does society promote desperousity, it engulfs us. To give you examples, let us look at one of our biggest media outlets - television. Take a sample of the programs currently on the air that not only promote but are talked about at work and on radio shows. The sad thing is that women are the biggest viewers to watch them, TV shows like "The Bachelorette", "The Bachelor", "Bridezilla", "Say Yes to the Dress", "My Fair Wedding" and other "so called" reality based TV shows highlighting women's needs and desires to get married.

Can we please get a grip? The other night, I was appalled watching a TV commercial for a show that had over twenty-five women, in bridal gowns, physically chasing a man down the street. Why? Because he was supposed to be such "a catch", and all of these women were supposed to embarrass, humiliate and lose all self-respect in fighting for his attentions. All this so he would "pick" them to be his bride in six weeks. What was appalling was that it seemed that most of these participants were beautiful, intelligent and successful women. Where was their self-esteem? Their self-respect? This disturbs me on so many levels as in this day and age society is still making us "desperate" for marriage.

Have we so quickly forgotten all the women who fought for women's rights, the right to own property, the right to vote, pay equity and so much more? Every time there is one needy or desperate woman, we are losing ground; the ground that so many brave women fought for so that we could live independent, free lives.

We, as women, have taken so many large movements forward and then we have this utter "crap" on TV for our young ladies to watch. The disturbing thing is that these shows get phenomenal ratings. Stop watching this "junk"! You are promoting women as stupid, useless cattle that are there for anyone as long as they will marry you. This to me is one of our biggest offenses of this century and if you watch it, you are supporting it. There is no reason for a woman to settle for, chase or think of just one guy when there are so many to "have" whenever she would like!

Oh my, can we please stop the DESPERATION??? Can we please NOT go into DESPEROUSITY???

Neediness. Desperation. Desperousity. Do not allow those feelings to make decisions for you. This is YOUR life we're talking about. Valuable years that need to be respected as time is the only thing that we can never get back.

Women can feel great freedom now! You don't have to feel that desperation as I did. We live in such an age of liberation and personal freedom. With this freedom, desperation should not push anyone into a quick, non-rewarding relationship. Yes, you can have whomever you want and not marry the one that you find distasteful because you are being pushed into a marriage. My goodness, you don't HAVE to marry anyone. If you feel that way, please get out of the relationship before your life ends up in divorce or you're filled with regrets from this obsolete ritual.

Being Married Does Not Bring Security

As the title of this chapter indicates, marriage does not bring security. Many people get married because they feel or believe that marriage will bring them emotional, financial and sexual security. For anyone that thinks this let me state plainly, "security" in any form is an illusion.

Let's review the definition of **illusion**: *The state of fact of being intellectually deceived or mislead.*

How often do we deceive ourselves? How often do we talk ourselves into or out of things? Both sexes are being unwise if they feel that marriage will give them any kind of security, especially for "the rest of their lives".

If you think getting married means that you are done – wake up! Marriage does not contain certainty. People that marry thinking that they will never be lonely again or that they will have someone forever and ever are under an illusion. The only constant in life is change. If anything, become secure in that fact.

Those seeking emotional security honestly ask yourselves, how many couples have you known have complained that after getting married that their lives became routine and monotonous. And that all the romance and courtship feelings are gone? The funny thing is that couples only have themselves to blame, as typically once a couple gets married they become complacent in their relationship figuring that they are done and don't have to make an effort anymore.

Let me ask, men are you still buying flowers for your wife or taking her out to dinner when it is not her birthday, your anniversary or Valentine's Day? Women are you still dressing in sexy lingerie and still giving him oral sex (I once heard a woman exclaim that now she was married she didn't have to give oral sex anymore – wrong and how selfish and foolish). Couples, what are you doing for each other to keep the relationship fresh, exciting and new? Or have you both just decided to take each other for granted?

In a marriage you are often under the illusion that you will be with each other forever and ever, and all too often couples get caught up in living life and lose the focus of their relationship. That is why you hear many married couples gripe about not having enough romance or emotional considerations. The fantastic thing about Partnership Agreements is that it keeps you on your toes, and cognizant of each other's needs, therefore forcing you to constantly take stock of your relationship, prioritize it and decide whether it emotionally works for you on a daily basis. If you know that your "contract" will end or be renewed in a certain amount of time, you will be on your best behavior and constantly focused on your relationship.

Many people marry thinking it will provide some

kind of financial security. Get a grip! I will not recount all the divorce horror stories about spouses that ran up secret debt and then stuck it to their spouse when they divorced. Or how many women have given up their careers to take care of the children full-time, only to wake up one day to find their husband has left them and they have to re-enter the job market with outdated skills or start at an entry level position. How about divorces that drag out and ruin a couple financially after the lawyers have taken their share from the divorce proceeding and custody battle. We have all heard some of these horror stories and yet, people still marry thinking it won't happen to them and without any protection.

A Partnership Agreement can avoid a lot of the financial stress that is associated with divorce and many other things. If you plan now for the possibility of dissolving your relationship in the future, then it will be less traumatic if or should it come to pass. Is it unromantic? Yes! Are you protecting yourself? Yes! Are you making sure that the "oxygen mask" is on you first? Heck yes! Remember these things are important. If you truly love each other and want to be together, make these arrangements NOW while your love is still strong, for it may change.

Ah, now marriage for fidelity. If anyone in his or her right mind thinks that marriage will prevent unfaithfulness from their partner, you need a reality check. A vow and ring does not guarantee monogamy! May I say again, in a contractual agreement he/she would be "choosing" to stay with you.

If you think that the only way you can keep your loved one near you and faithful to you is with an "I do", then don't. If at your engagement party you are sizing up the best man, or the maid of honor, or their dates and wondering if you could get them in the sack before you get married - do not get married or contracted. Simply, question your intentions. Question your motives. And most importantly, do you really feel you could be faithful to this man or woman for the REST OF YOUR LIFE? HOW IN THE HELL COULD ANYONE KNOW THE ANSWER TO THAT QUESTION??? OR MAYBE YOU ARE SAYING, WHY ARE THEY MAKING ME SWEAR TO THAT???

Security in marriage is not spelled out. In contracts, you at least have an idea of what each other expects as it is written down and no one has to guess or assume. Some people believe that security and maturity go hand in hand. I believe that maturity is over-rated. I much prefer living in my mind of fun and games, but that's just who I am. I feel life is serious enough and knocks the hell out of us in so many ways that it is time we realize that life is challenging enough; therefore we need as much playfulness as possible in all other ways. Contracts allow us the room to share our challenges and see if we can pull through them in five-year increments. If not, there should be no blame, just adjustment to the new people that we have become. New people seasoned to the joys and traumas of life. People who know how they want to spend their moments.

You see a contract doesn't mean you will not support your partner, it just means that you will find it easier to let go or re-up at the time of renewal. These contracts don't and can't change what life brings us, but they can help us with self-examination and honesty with others, and most importantly with ourselves. This would be the greatest security we can have. The security that we find within ourselves.

If you want security, make it contractual financial security and stop looking for security that comes from love. Love IS. It is out there for us to partake. Love is infinite and when we bring it into our lives it is beautiful. Many people fall under the illusion that when they take their marriage vows, they feel their love is different and their marriage will survive the 50% divorce rate. It might not. Sad to say the odds are against you. Take the pressure off yourself. We can choose to love one person for the rest of our lives, but we don't have to swear to it...just do it.

Monogamy, A Natural State of Being?

I believe that monogamy is not a natural state of being – for men and women. The end.

No, just kidding.

We can revisit my earlier chapter on marriage and when ancient people lived in tribes. Sex among early humans was communal and occurred with different partners to assure that the tribe was populated and strong. No one was concerned with who was sleeping with whom because ancient people didn't practice monogamy.

Remember, marriage and monogamy only came into existence to assure the paternity of a child to pass on land, property, kingdoms and other inheritances.

So what does that have to do with the NOW?

I would like men and woman to explore the idea that we may not be wired to be with one person for the rest of our lives. Marriage and monogamy may be seen as an unnatural state. I am not saying that we shouldn't be together with just one person in our lives; I am saying that we need to look at not promising, making an oath or commitment to and in front of anyone that we stay monogamous.

When will we accept that sex is a huge part of who we are?

I do feel that men are following nature to be sexually uninhibited. I am not saying that men lack control of their bodies, but I think we can all acknowledge that men's sexual drive is profoundly strong and part of their biology. However, this does not have societal consequences unless they become predators.

Women, I think we are equally as naturally uninhibited sexually as well but do not act on it easily. Society and those who have rule over women have conditioned us to believe that we are not and should not be sexually active. Even recently, a male radio host called a woman a "slut" for wanting to have the rights just to take birth control.

When it comes to sex, it is simple. Women and men are not complicated. Really, all that men want from the moment they discover their penis is to have someone else touch it and if no one else will, they will keep their own hands on it. Men feel it is something to be played with and a lot of men can't understand why a woman wouldn't want to play with it all the time. After all, a man feels that if he were a woman, he would have a great time playing with himself as a woman all day!

I am a healthy sexual woman and I can't understand why women wouldn't want sex with multiple partners. If you find one man that you can get emotionally involved with and he takes you to a divine place sexually, then go for it. However, if you want to explore, do so.

My point on monogamy is that I feel men choose to be monogamous and women want to be monogamous. Women typically equate sex with love and most men DO NOT equate sex with love. Men want to have sex with their love. Usually, it is the man that wants sex either way.

It is a hard concept for women to understand that men often see sex as merely an act, because women equate sex with love. It is difficult for some women to accept having casual sex without any emotions involved in the act, because women are fearful of the stigma attached to their actions. Yet, men can freely express their sexuality without judgments or labels. I hope that women now feel free to partake in these sexual freedoms as well.

I am stating what I feel, and that exploring our sexuality is a part of our spiritual desire to know and experience. Judgment lies within the earth plane not in the realm of spirituality. Spirituality is based on experiences, not judgments. I understand that this is a hard concept for people to understand. Our reluctance to understand comes from a long history of religion and society sitting as dictator of our lives. Many of us have learned that religion and society do not allow us to hold our hearts freely. Freedom comes from the Universal Truths that resonate within us through our own individual spirituality.

Metaphysically speaking, monogamy could be considered a misinterpretation of the power of our energies that create our physical forms. We humans are still connected on some level. A connection that makes us feel a strong desire to link together, to form alliances with each other that are both societal and individual. It is within spirituality that we discuss the need to have conscious awareness, respect and compassion for all things. To find joy in the nothingness and to have awareness for all that is present and non-present. We join our vibrations in the most beautiful of acts — intercourse of the sexes. The Universe doesn't judge this, so why should we? This also means that no one should be shocked or surprised by our need for each other. If we decide and choose to share our sexuality with only one person, of course, that too is respected. Make no mistake, when it comes to rape or physical abuse that is a crime against the individual and society. Consensual sex is not.

Please note, that with changing roles with men and women in society, many men are facing less and less stigma about expressing their emotions. More and more men are becoming emotional about sex and actively choosing to be monogamous and enjoying commitment. Women, you may need to make sure that HE isn't expecting more from you then you are ready to give. Men and women, don't promise you will be monogamous if you know that you can't be!

Interestingly, once the taboo is lifted on both sexes to be free to enjoy multiple partners, the cosmic joke will be that we will crave being with just one person. The old human characteristic of wanting something that is different. If it isn't taboo anymore, than it isn't as much fun. Hmmm, that may be true for some, but I still feel we will want to play in the fields of experiential sexuality. I am not speaking of deviant behavior, and we cannot judge what is "deviant" to another UNLESS it is done to someone without their consent. Even just a "kiss" may be considered perverse if done without consent. That also goes for sexual language and suggestive remarks.

Sex is just a great thing! Even the most diehard among us can't keep ourselves from swooning over that one great man or woman, that just made us feel hot, sexy, beautiful and desirable and we want him/her all to ourselves. However, men in a couple of hours may start thinking, "now where can I go for some new excitement" or he may be sound asleep. She may be planning centerpieces for the wedding or picking names for their first born.

When it comes to monogamy, men and women need to be brutally honest with each other. If not, you are creating a lot of pain down the road and being an outright liar to yourself and your partner. If either of you do not believe you can stay monogamous with a partner, then DO NOT promise that you will. However, if you say you are going to be monogamous for a year and you are not, then you should have consequences. No excuses!

If your partner states that they "love you", but they cannot commit to you, there should be no judgment. You should accept that your partner is being honest with you about their wants, needs, desires and even limitations. You should respect that they are being honest with you and not leading you astray. Even if this is not the scenario that you wanted, you should view it as a loving and respectful statement of one's true feelings. Honor this! It is better than having them lie to you and telling you what you wanted to hear. They took the harder path of honesty knowing that they will hurt you a little rather than hurt a lot with a betrayal.

If your partner has told you that they cannot be faithful, you now need to be honest with yourself and decide if you can accept that, or CHOOSE to leave the relationship. If you love this person and are willing to accept that they will not be monogamous in your relationship, then you have to ACCEPT this! DO NOT think that you can change their mind now or later. It will not happen. If you accept this relationship, than you must learn how to keep your emotions intact, especially if you are with a lover that has stated they have no intention of being monogamous with you.

Please do not think that marriage or a contract can or will bring you everything, only open and honest communication can. Explore who you are sexually, think about marriage versus contracts and enjoy your life experiences the best you can while growing from your own physical/spiritual center.

Monogamy Should Be A Choice Not A Judgment By Society

In our time on this planet, we have seen, read, and have been polarized and condemning of anyone that cheats. We say it is immoral or they lose character because he or she has affairs. Who has placed these moral standards on us? Yes, if you promise someone something, you should follow through. That does show integrity and character.

Now we know that robbing a bank is considered a crime against society. That leads us to think that anyone who has committed this crime as immoral, or has a lack of character or integrity. However, if someone "cheats" on a spouse, this is not a crime against society but a broken vow that they had made at the time of wedlock. Society actually cares little about any affair unless that person is in the limelight of celebrity. Then it is just fodder for all the voyeurs in our world. You usually won't get more than an eyebrow raised from anyone outside of your immediate family or circle of friends. Most friends don't care if you are cheating, as long as it isn't with their spouse! All of us in some way are hypocritical. Again, it is part of the human being.

Depending on the size of your celebrity will determine how harshly you will be criticized from a society that has no business being in anyone's private life in the first place. Then society typically will say, "He/She is an icon and a mentor for our youth and we need to have responsible people in these roles." Maybe we should figure out that celebrities, sports figures, political officials and anyone in the public eye, should not be "required" to carry the onus of being super human let alone the icons of our youth.

Since sex is a natural part of our being, it would not be news if someone had multiple partners if we could get ourselves out of these puritanical thought processes. Sex is no different than any other bodily function, however it is a lot more fun than most of them.

If we can advertise in the media, condoms, Viagra, personal lubricants and other personal items that usually have to do with sex and getting a sexual partner, then we should be able to accept sexuality and people's sexual escapades without a fuss.

As the voyeurs that we are, we are pinned to our TV for news about sexual adventures of anyone and yet we dare to criticize, cajole and judge those who want to live a sexually stimulating life. Shame on us society. It is time to stop being so hypocritical. Most of us love sex and anything that has to do with it. We have been programmed that way since we crawled out of the slime and it is about time we get used to it.

Maybe we should finally start to realize that to be human means that monogamous behavior cannot exist along with other demands made upon us by society. I reiterate, monogamy is a choice people make everyday in many ways. Let us accept that we do not own another person's life, dreams, fantasies and desires.

With the definitions of the words, "morality, integrity, character", we can see that it all depends on what "we" consider these "principles of conduct" to be. Society judges this or that as moral or immoral, but why is society the end all of what is moral, has integrity or character? We judge other societies all the time. Does anyone remember when we called Native Americans, heathens? Unfortunately, I'm sure that some people still do. However, many of us now see that Native Americans have many interesting traditions that we like, celebrate and pursue.

WE CHANGE! Society changes. Things that we considered immoral previously, we do not look at the same way - divorce for one. There was a time that you didn't divorce. It was not condoned by society, and many women became outcasts if they were a "divorcee". A word that was parallel to being a whore or failure.

I feel that holding any person to go against their natural desire, such as having a lot of sexual activity, would be going against the basic character of the human being. We should not hold anyone to some harsh standard, unless you consider judgment and righteousness reasons for having such standards.

This is ludicrous. Most human beings have multiple partners so why do such standards exist? We are a closed minded society. We are more comfortable pretending that sexual activity with multiple partners doesn't exist. Yet, at the same time, we are used to marriages falling apart because of infidelity.

We need to look at why in our society we penalize people for doing the things that are the norm for our basic needs and support of our psyche. Yes, one of these things that may be good for our personal needs could be multiple physical partners. You do not have to participate in this; just relieve the judgment put upon others that do pursue this lifestyle.

Yet, we have bought into the concept of marriage and monogamy. We not only brought it into this century, but have thrust it upon each other as a badge of duty and honor. And when it all goes wrong, some poor person (male or female) feels they have let their partner, family, and the world down. They accuse themselves of a lack of integrity, lack of character, morally indecent, on and on. What they are not realizing is that by getting married in the first place and expecting monogamy from either partner is actually the lack of integrity. It takes integrity to say up front, I don't know if I can stay monogamous "forever", however, for the next five years I will agree to do so.

Please do not say to me, "well that is too bad, they made their choices and they need to live with it". Any of us who have been there know that it isn't about facing some ideal that we place upon ourselves stating that being miserable is righteous. This is pure foolishness. Hopefully, we will stop this thinking and find our way to choosing a full and sexually stimulated life. We need NOT to make generalities about people concerning their integrity, moral fiber or character. Every day, every moment in time is a choice. How do you want to use your choices today?

This is why contracts need to exist. If people were given the freedom to make choices about monogamy, moment-by-moment, contract-by-contract, rather than "forever" as in a marriage, this could alleviate the feelings of guilt, blame, shame or stigma when a partner wants to leave a relationship because they don't want to be monogamous anymore. I feel that no one should feel guilty or carry fault, because they are responding to their own needs and feelings. To deny that, reeks of old religion and judgments of good and bad. We are all good and bad. We are all perfect imperfect beings. That is what makes us all so remarkably wonderful and deliciously funny.

Part Two

The Contract

The Contract/Partnership Agreement should help all people, but particularly those who are in lust instead of love. I feel that if it takes a great deal to get INTO THE partnership, it may prevent people from frivolous, lust driven, romantic fantasies that are not real. Or, hopefully they can be brought into reality with probing questions from each other, their mediators or lawyers about finances, children, religion, vacations, living arrangements, etc.

When you are first entering a partnership is when you are most vulnerable as you still think the sun shines out your partner's ass. After spending a great deal of time, intimacy and child rearing with this person, you come back down to earth and that is when reality can hit you hard. Thus, the need to be thinking straight at the beginning of the contract is important. Then after the signing of the contract is when you can get frivolous, lusty and romantic. Remember to keep that part alive.

I totally and completely believe in contracts, but NOT marriage contracts, as that wants you to put your life into the hands of someone else. Nothing is based on individuality in marriage. It becomes we and us forever. That should scare you.

A Partnership Contract will force couples to address their individual needs before committing to each other. You have to learn what you will and won't compromise on as well as learn from your potential partner what they will and won't compromise on.

For instance, I had a friend of mine that informed her partner, before they committed, that she would never ever live in the southern part of the U.S. with humidity or in the northern part of the U.S. with snow and negative temperatures. She was a west, southwest, warm weather girl and that was not going to change. She told her partner she would never be happy in those places and she would not move there. It was a point she could not compromise on and she wanted her partner to know before they committed.

And that is what I am talking about, before you commit, you need to find out from each other exactly what are the issues or needs that you can and cannot compromise on during your relationship. And please, do not think you can change the other's mind during the course of your relationship. If she only wants one child and you want four, do not think she will change her mind and want more after she has the first baby. You are ignoring your partner's needs as well as your own needs. If you really, really want four kids, then you need to find someone who will share in the joy and happiness of raising four children with you. Not living with the disappointment of only having one child with your partner. Be realistic now, not miserable and unhappy later.

We could benefit from the seriousness of a contract, which is based on real, earth plane existence compared to a marriage contract, which is based on the romantic idea of two individuals loving each other until one, or the other leaves this world.

We need to get with the times and energies that exist in this earth plane at this moment. That is the fact that we know more about sex 'n' love than ever before, so let us all get down to the nitty-gritty. We don't need to get married to keep the money in the family, save nations from ruin or keep a monarchy strong. What we need now is freedom of will and choice.

I suggest and will continue to suggest to people, that if you are in love and want to share life together, then you should enter a Partnership Contract. This is an agreement, not a traditional marriage. I feel we should be talking about the dissolution of marriage and putting our expectations, financial arrangements, having or not having children, guardianship, vacations, time alone, family, family visits and anything else that is important to both parties down on paper. It's about boundaries and it's about being clear on what each person wants and expects from the relationship.

In a marriage contract, you go and get a license from a city hall (which is just a way of registering your marriage to make it lawful), if religious you go and get a religious ceremony set up, you get dresses, tuxedos, a caterer, a hall or ballroom, go through all the hoopla and whatevers and *if smart*, whether you have money or not, you get a prenuptial agreement. After that, you live everyday with a gnawing question in the back of your mind; did I do the right thing for me?

If you are just a guy and a gal, with no means of supporting yourself, don't get married. Get a contract! Remember, two cannot live as cheaply as one. Be optimistic and make provisions in case one of you strikes it rich!

If you are a wealthy man and a wealthy woman and you want to live together, don't get married. Before living with each other, go to the lawyers and set up a contract with all your assets being put forth and coming to agreements before you sign on the dotted line.

If you are a wealthy man and want to live with a woman who is not bringing wealth to the table, have an agreement as to what you think is fair in terms of financial arrangements during and possibly after the relationship. Be precise and don't be stupid. That is why you will have a lawyer and the partner will have a different lawyer to protect each of your interests.

If you are a wealthy woman and want a contract with a man that is not wealthy, have an agreement as to what you think is fair in terms of financial arrangements during and possibly after the relationship. Again, be precise and don't be stupid. That is why you will have a lawyer and the partner will have a lawyer.

We are not perfect beings, thus the contracts won't be perfect, but I guarantee that couples will be better represented by a contract then to just get up in front of a huge group of people saying, "I do" ... and better for all. These contracts will not be "forever"... only for five-years, and like all contracts they can be changed, amended or reexamined at any time.

The same goes for homosexual couples. Don't get married. Except some of the time gay marriages work much better for those involved, probably because they had to work so hard at being able to marry that they come into it with different expectations and respect, but still, please get contracted not married.

In case you have not gotten my point so far, even though marriage is a contract, it is NOT the contract I suggest anyone get into... DO NOT GET A MARRIAGE CONTRACT!!! GET AN INDIVIDUAL CONTRACT, A PARTNERSHIP AGREEMENT, THAT IS DRAWN UP BY A LAWYER OR MEDIATOR THAT COVERS YOU BOTH INDIVIDUALLY AND AS A COUPLE AND FORGET MARRIAGE.

Just as a side note, for all the mothers and fathers that want to see their kids get married and feel this type of arrangement cheats you out of seeing your kids get married, I suggest this:

Go to the lawyer with your kids when they sign the contract. All of you will walk out with a lot more money than throwing that wedding. Then after the signing, let your kids go to a party where everyone can celebrate and can just look to get drunk and laid. Or, parents watch your kids sign the papers and then go to the bar and meet your friends for a drink on you. Or, have a Contract Reception that is a huge party and provides all the frou-frou you want including tuxedos, gowns, contract rings and champagne. Your choice!

To those who would say that we don't have to have all the hoopla and we can just have a civil ceremony, are missing my point. You are not protected as an individual and you are still vowing to stay together "forever" or "until death do you part". I am stating: be radical, get rid of marriage!

Okay, back to contracts and why I feel we should have them instead of marriage. We need to have a contracted society and not a marriage society. My idea for Partnership Contract is based on two people getting together with each of their individual lawyers or mediators, having them draw up a contract and meeting to make it an official document in regards to the wishes of the individuals, within the contractual agreement and not what society, religion or family wants us to commit to. Marriage with this "until death do we part" crap is for undying fanatical romantics and does not work in our current times. I can promise you, if you knew a contract was coming up in a few years and you were either going to go on in continued contentment or get dumped, a lot would change in the house as we know it.

If society moved toward Partnership Contracts, without the religious connotations of marriage, we would relieve a great amount of guilt, self-destruction and unhappiness for many people. In all due respect to those that think that a Partnership Agreement is an easy way out, it is not. It may make it easier than a divorce, which it is designed to do, but what it does bring to the table is accountability. And accountability should take the place of out of date standards.

With a contract, the courts would still work out any disputes in mediation. If mediation doesn't work, the courts would hear any disputes just like any business contract. I would likely wager that most courts would see a large drop in their domestic squabbles in Family Court, as I am advocating that the dissolution of your relationship would be planned ahead of time.

By the way, I am not a lawyer and do not receive any benefits from lawyers, mediators or lawyer/mediator groups. I am a pragmatist that wants us to start to get into the NOW of our lives and get away from getting ourselves into situations that bring us such pain. If you are happy in your contract, all you have to do is re-up and keep living on in fabulous joy.

My experiences have been in my own failed marriages along with my intuitive metaphysical training. My intuitive abilities have been sought out by people and they have allowed me into their lives to hear their deepest woes and sincerest wishes, not only to be in love, but to also remain in lust. All of this has been accompanied by their desire to be wealthy, healthy and perfect. It has been my experience that often the difference between a failed relationship and a successful relationship is communication, boundaries and honesty. That is what a Contract Agreement is forcing couples to do - be honest with each other and to communicate expectations and parameters. Then couples can have the freedom to play, sex it up and just enjoy each other! They can have "An almost perfect little picture in a very imperfect world."

Length of the Contract

I want to reiterate, get your mind out of the use of the term "marriage contract". The contract that I am speaking of is a formal, legal contract such as the one that you will see used in business transactions. It is legal disclosures of the "whats" that you will do and "whats" that your partner will do, how you will settle your differences along with disclosing the truthful monetary worth of each partner, and the conditions of the eventual raising of children.

From my personal experience, I have concluded that five years is an appropriate amount of time for the first contract. For example: the first year we fall all over each other trying to please our partner and adjust to living with each other. By the second year, we start to lose the lust effect and start to think about career, family and maybe a bigger home. By the third year we may want or already have children, more responsibility, a bigger mortgage, etc. By the fourth year, we are feeling pretty comfortable with each other and we start to deal with relationship routine and how to keep our relationship fresh and alive. The fifth year we use to evaluate our situations and ourselves, performing a lot of introspection and assessing our arrangement.

Understand that you can draw up your contract for as long or as short as you would like it to be. I just happen to have the experience of knowing that most people start to fall out of lust/love by the fifth year of being together. That is why I say five years. It is based purely on my opinion. _The individuals involved should set all terms of the contract._ I would hope that you would choose a lawyer or mediator that will ensure that all of your concerns are covered in the agreement.

WE SHOULD HAVE FIVE-YEAR CONTRACTS THAT WE SIGN AND BY THE END OF THOSE FIVE YEARS, IF YOU WANT TO SIGN UP FOR ANOTHER FIVE YEARS, SO BE IT. IF NOT, YOU WILL BOTH LEAVE THE SITUATION BY THE CONTENTS OF THE

SIGNED CONTRACT NO MATTER WHO IS UNHAPPY
WITHIN THE CONTRACTED AGREEMENT.

Children and the Contract

The biggest question whenever I speak of contracts
usually is: But what about the children? What about
them? You contract the same way when you have
children as when you negotiated the contract about
living together. He takes the kids. She takes the kids.
The grandparents get the kids whenever and
whatever the contract says. So many kids today are
brought up in divorced homes anyway; half of the
kids in America are already living with contracted
parents. So really what is the difference?

Think about it, with a Partnership Contract versus a
marriage contract, you are actually being proactive
in thinking about and planning for your children's
well being, especially during what could be a time of
great emotional stress if you and your partner
decide to part ways. Why would you want a court
judge deciding your children's visitation or anything
else about your children?

I strongly advocate that while the both of you are
still in love to plan as much as possible for the well-
being of the children. Your goal is to protect them

from any irrational reactions, hurt, resentment and the "gonna get you back" emotional attitude should either one of you break the contractual agreement. This contract safeguards the children before your love turns to hate.

In the contract, you will need to address the dual roles each parent will assume during the relationship and possibly after the relationship dissolves. It should also include: who gets what type of custody, if and when the grandparents may visit and where, schools preferred, how financial support will be divided between each parent for all expenses including insurance premiums, who would be guardians in case of death of both parents, and who will be receiving funds from insurance and estates to provide for the children. Yes, you could go on and on hopefully you get the point. Again, you need to address any issues that you find important to your child's upbringing in advance so it doesn't become a point of contention in the future.

Keep in mind, life changes and this might be the section of the contract that will be modified the most as you add children to your family, and as they get older. You may have to go back to this clause yearly.

If one of the partners chooses to stay home with the children, this must be spelled out. Will the other partner reimburse the parent giving up job opportunities to take care of the children? What about retirement savings while a parent is home with the children? What other financial arrangements must be addressed? Please do not take this lightly. Make sure that everything that you feel is important for the future of your children and for yourself is in the contract.

An added bonus to having a contract, is that hopefully we would have couples that are staying in shape (maybe), that would watch their manners, not take each other for granted, would have an active and healthy sex life (hopefully), no dominating, no ownership, just two people that are really living it up. Then when the kids arrive, the children will understand that every five years their parents will re-evaluate their goals for the entire family. This should include the parent's desire for each other. The contract will give couples the freedom to change their contract, re-up it or dissolve it, and whatever choice they make, they will have solace in knowing that their children are protected.

Money

Money is extremely important in your contract. I cannot stress it enough. The two things that couples fight about the most are sex and money.

MONEY -- Put it on paper...ALL of it. Not just where you are now with money but where you might be some day.

First, you both must write down what each is bringing into the contract. Money, stocks, bonds, retirement accounts, interest, property, possessions (jewelry, furs, etc.) investments, debt and profit(s) from occupations. If you are both without assets, make provisions in your contract for when assets may be acquired as life changes and so will your financial status. You need to decide what you want to merge together in your partnership and what you want to keep separate.

If either partner does not want to be totally open and honest about what they have and/or are not willing to disclose these things in a contract, _then do not enter into a contract with them._ You can remain single with your finances and investments intact and just see each other, but do not give up your house or apartment and move in with them. Do not share housing or bank accounts. Do not take up residence with anyone that will not enter into a contract with you. Do not have children with someone that won't contract with you about the children's welfare and financial future.

If you are struggling and don't have enough money at the moment, you need a contract before you enter a partnership. Now some would say, "I don't have enough money for a lawyer or mediator." Then you have NO business moving in together! Get your affairs in order. How can you take into account the needs of someone else if you can't even take care of your own needs?

First off, you shouldn't be living together if you don't have enough money. Some couples will anyway, so at least be prepared with a contract. Why leave yourself vulnerable to another person? What happens when you come home one day and have found that your home has been cleaned out, your partner has left and your bank account is empty? What recourse do you have? None! You didn't protect yourself. Get a contract folks!

When looking at money, take into account all situations and scenarios such as, what happens if one partner gets rich and the other goes broke? Investment issues need to be taken into account. If one partner uses all of their money for a down payment on a home and later the home is sold because of a break-up, who receives the proceeds and is there interest on the money involved? If one person comes to the partnership with a lot of debt, is the other partner willing to take on that burden or be excluded from it? What about money for the children? Do you set up a trust for the children? At what ages should they receive it? Guardianship -- who will be and what will they be paid? As for the executor of your will, who will it be and how much of your estate do they get? If everyone in your family hates your partner and you die, how do you protect your partner from your family that wants to take your estate away from them?

Consider ALL the what ifs!

This is just a small sample of all the financial concerns that need to be addressed before you enter a Partnership Contract.

You see, when you are in the first stages of love, these things seem unimportant. Then after a few months, when the bills start rolling in, then you start having discussions about debt and who pays what and how to get yourselves out of it. Then it is too late. It is one of the biggest issues that will break-up relationships faster than any other reason.

Some additional questions to ask about money: Who is going to cover the debt? What are you willing to give up per chance one of you or both of you should lose a job? Should the partner work weekends to make up for the lost income? Whose car do you sell? How many jobs are you willing to work if you want your partner to stay home with the children? How much time will you be given on weekends to be with the children if you are working three jobs? How much time should both partners put into work? And on and on and on.

Debt and bankruptcy seem to go hand-in-hand with break-ups. You may be in love with each other when you start out, but by the time the bill collectors are chasing you down, romance and passion goes right out the window. You will hardly be able to even look at your partner without rage, especially if this debt isn't yours. It is imperative that these issues are talked about and written down in the contract. You will hear that famous statement: "if you loved me you wouldn't ask these things of me," and don't any of you dare fall for that one. If you love each other you will be concerned that each other is happy with the financial situation, whether you are together or not. It is a form of respect and love to make sure your financial arrangements are part of the contract. No ifs, ands or buts about it!

Don't forget your Last Will and Testament along with a Living Will to take care of your wishes. Talk about and arrange, with great care, any provisions in regards to catastrophic health circumstances or long-term illnesses that may arise within your contract. Many couples fail to discuss this very important and touchy subject, until the worst case scenario happens and they are often ill prepared for it. Help protect your partner and yourself by making sure all your wishes are accounted for and documented. This way you do not leave your partner vulnerable to family squabbles or legal litigation.

Work on this part of your contract with your partner. Write everything down and then take the agreement to your <u>individual</u> lawyer/mediator to review it and make adjustments while your loved one isn't there. Your lawyer/mediator will go over all contract topics and may ask additional questions to help protect you. They will talk to you frankly, which is invaluable as you will be sitting there with stars in your eyes, lust in your loins and you will give away the estate along with everything in it.

Then you and your lawyer can present these adjustments when all of you are together and changes and compromises can be made with as little drama as possible. Or, have lots of drama! Whatever excites you is fine with me.

Understanding the part of life that is involved in making money, investing money, spending money, saving money and using your smarts in creating a good contract, will hopefully keep the drama low. If you do not do this because you just don't want to talk about money as in, "he or she is just the cutest little thing and wouldn't do anything to ever hurt little ole' me, ever"-- is a delusion. You need someone to help you keep perspective as you may not have any during this time.

Nothing can actually keep you from the unexpected. There is always the unexpected. However, going into a contract with as much knowledge as possible is a good foundation from which to work. Remember, nothing is perfect and your contract won't be either. But your protection is paramount and you need to remember that!

Always know where you are financially. If one partner is doing all of the taxes, bill paying and paperwork, you sit down with them once a week to look at where you are in regards to the money -- what you have coming in and what is going out. _Do not leave one person in charge of finances while you walk around ignorant._ If that partner dies or just walks out on you one day, you could be left with a huge mess, one of unfathomable repercussions. At the very least, always look at the bottom line and ask questions! It is always better to be informed than to be ignorant.

Expectations

Expectations are a HUGE part of your contract! Often

we go through life with expectations for ourselves and for other people, but rarely do we communicate or express our expectations to each other. We then find ourselves angry or upset because others are not living up to our expectations, when in reality these people have no idea of your expectations for them. Besides, they have their own expectations for themselves that may not coincide with your expectations.

It is important when outlining your contract and in any relationship in general, that you express what your expectations are for yourself and for your partner. Open dialogue and communication are key. This way everyone is speaking the same language and there is none of this, "well they should know why I am angry..." silliness going on. Trust me ladies, men cannot read your minds. You have to talk to each other and tell each other what you want!

Before we delve into expectations, I do want to briefly mention that communicating expectations is very, very, very important, but if you are not able to accept an expectation - DO NOT GET CONTRACTED! Do not accept an expectation your partner sets forth thinking that you can change it down the road. Respect your partner's wants, needs and desires, as well as your own, and if you are not able to - then do not get contracted, and vice-versa for you as well. If your partner is not willing to accept an expectation of yours - DO NOT GET CONTRACTED!

You have to accept each other "as is". Think of it as that house you buy. It is all you can afford and you hope that fixing it up will be fun and suit your needs for the time being. However, when you expect your partner to change to suit yourself is when you get in trouble. For example, if they are overweight and you expect them to slim down, trouble. If your partner doesn't like sex and you think they will change, trouble. If body parts are not to your liking and you feel they will pursue surgery or other means, trouble. If breasts or a penis is not to your liking, it will not get better with age. Before you enter any Partnership Contract you need to accept your partner for who they are and not what you want them to become. Don't fall in love with the potential of a person, fall in love with who they truly are.

Monogamy: This is a section that you need to be completely honest with each other and not say the things that you think that your partner wants to hear. How monogamous can you be?

Would you, could you, agree to an open relationship where you would have sexual relationships with others with no consequences? Or, how long do you feel as an individual that you can stay monogamous - - one year, two years, five years, etc. If you contract to stay monogamous, then you need to keep that promise or face the consequences that have been agreed upon.

What are the consequences if one of you should break that promise? Define the consequences. Define the outcome of the consequences. Counseling? Or is this the end of the contract/ relationship?

Monogamy is often assumed and rarely discussed. It would be beneficial to both parties if you think long and hard about "if" you can stay monogamous. I suggest strongly, that it be imperative for you both to tackle the point of whether you expect or desire your partner to be monogamous. The consequences for infidelity need to be spelled out, if or when this may occur for either party within this partnership. This acknowledges that you are aware that monogamy is a choice and you both enter this agreement with eyes wide open.

Cold, calculated, no romantic overtures—you betcha! This is the time to put your feet on the ground. You can wait to float on the clouds once the contract has been signed.

Sex: Thank goodness in this day and age we can finally talk very openly about what we want and need from each other sexually, which is great for today's couples.

I mentioned before that the two things that couples fight about most is, money and SEX! Be honest with each other about what you want sexually. For example, do you enjoy oral sex? How often do you want sex? Do you have a strong libido? Do you like kissing? What about PDA (public displays of attention)? How much? How little?

Basically, what do you want sexually from each other and how often? Yes, it needs to be discussed. How often are you doin' it? Do you want to do it more or less? Are you happy? Is there something sexually you want to try? Do either one of you have a fetish? Are you into role playing? And I could go on and on, but you get the picture.

It is important to respect your partner's expression of sexual desires and needs, and to respect your own desires and needs as well. Respect is necessary no matter what type of relationship you are in. Do not belittle your partner's sexual fantasies or desires. This is important to them and it should be important to you. Having open and honest discussions without judgment is paramount to a beneficial relationship. You may not want some of this in the contract, but it is an excellent discussion to have with each other.

Sex is so very, very, very important in a relationship

and not just for the man. You need to be clear with each other on what is desired and needed. You need to be willing to give to each other to be sexually fulfilled. This does not mean either one of you can't be spontaneous, but so many couples do not have an open dialogue about their sexual needs. Talk about it people! Our sexuality is such a fabulous gift, do not squander it. Enjoy each other. Explore each other. Do each other. Have fun!

Physical Beauty/Lifestyle: I bring this up because there are such different views on beauty and what is considered beautiful as well as physical lifestyle. You need to be clear on it as a couple. I feel that today's couples do not maintain their physical attraction to one another. The whole point of these contracts is to keep couples on their toes and keep them from taking each other for granted, not just emotionally but physically as well.

Before you enter the contract, you need to address what your expectations are in regards to physical beauty and lifestyle. For instance, does he expect her to stay blonde? Does he expect her to get a boob job because he likes big breasts? Does she not want him to have facial hair? Will she accept a beer belly? Does she expect him to stop playing inter-mural sports when they are together? Do you expect them to stop smoking or drinking less? Do you expect him not to go out with the boys anymore? Does he object to a night out with the girls?

All the expectations that you have for each other in your heads need to be verbalized and communicated to your partner. If you are fine with each other sitting on the couch, growing fat and playing video games, great as long as you are both fine with it. However, there are many people that want their partner to stay physically fit and they may put a clause in their contract about weight gain. Again, just be clear and honest about your needs, wants, desires and expectations! I cannot stress it enough.

Sickness & Health: This is an expectation that is often overlooked. Couples just assume that during an illness, be it physical, mental or both, a partner will be there for them and support them through it. This is not always the case. If there are significant health issues that change your lifestyle, you may need to state whether you can handle your loved one in a position of sickness.

You need to establish whether you can handle a mental illness, physical illness, both or neither. Some people have a difficult time dealing with a mental illness versus a physical one or vice-versa. Does a mental illness include addiction or not? Are you going to be able to handle a long-term illness or disability?

Do not care about how it sounds if you honestly state that you cannot handle an illness. If you truly love and respect each other you should be openly honest about this.

This is also something that needs to be reviewed in the financial portion of your contract in terms of disability insurance, life insurance, etc.

Also, do not discount sickness and health in regards to the children's portion of your contract should you choose to have them. Coming together to raise a family is filled with responsibility, but also joy.

Behavior: In the beginning of this chapter I brought up accepting your partner "as is" and trying not to fix them up or change them. It is so important that you appreciate each other's individuality. Then your partnership will become one of respect and love, thus building on what makes each of you wonderful and different, while accepting each other's flaws and limitations. This is so true with behavior.

If there is a behavior you do not like in each other, do not automatically assume that this behavior will end once you are contracted. You need to address any behaviors that you find so annoying that it could prevent you from entering a contract now, rather than end a contract later.

I personally feel women fail at adequately expressing their annoyance with their partner's behavior, or live under the illusion that it will all change once they live together. This is not the time to be polite or shy. Be frankly honest with each other. There is no point on hiding anything in fear that they may leave or not contract with you, as everything will soon be out in the open when you are living with each other 24/7. Get everything out on the table NOW!

Ok ladies! Does it drive you crazy that he spends four hours a day playing video games? Do you hate that he has his Blackberry at the dining table and uses it during dinner? Does it bug you that he only showers once a week? Seriously, get it all out and discuss it before it festers and you become resentful and bitter.

Same for you boys, what is it about her that you need to deal with before you get contracted? What is it that makes you clench your jaw? Does she make that weird disproving face every time you go out with a certain friend? Do you hate the way she leaves her shoes all over the house? Does it make you nuts that she takes so long primping that you are constantly late to everything?

Listen ladies and gentleman, you have to discuss these behaviors prior to getting contracted. These behaviors or traits are not going to change without discussion. The bonus is that you both may learn a big lesson about compromise, tolerance, and what behaviors you are willing to live with and what you are not. It is about setting boundaries. If it is that important to you, get it on paper; otherwise learn to live with it until the next contract.

Addictions: I personally feel that drug abuse, alcoholism and gambling addictions are deal breakers. However this has to be an individual decision, but I strongly urge that you protect yourself against addiction in your relationship.

I would recommend having a direct statement in the contract that would dissolve the relationship in the event of these abusive behaviors. Please, don't live under the illusion that this may never happen in your relationship. It may not happen, but then again it may. Either way, you may find solace in the fact you are protected. Don't ignore any addictive behavior at the beginning of your relationship not wanting to face that it is an addiction. None of these behaviors will disappear once you are contracted, in fact they will become more prominent once you are living together. Deal with it NOW!

Home & Living: This is a commonly overlooked topic between couples as often couples assume that they both want the same thing. It is not until they are together that they then discover that one doesn't have the same dream of living in New York. Or, one doesn't want that farm in the country. The simple concept of "where" to live is often never discussed, and folks it is a big one. Before entering a contract, be clear on WHERE you want to live from house, condo and apartment to city, town or country.

Vacation & Holidays: While discussing home and living, talk about where you want to vacation and how you are going to spend the holidays. Do you both like to take vacations? What do you do when one does and the other doesn't? Does he want to go to the same place every year and you want to go somewhere different every year? Does she like to relax and he wants an adventure vacation? Get straight on how you want to spend your precious and hard earned vacation days. Talk about it now, before it becomes a point of contention.

And while we are on vacations, let's not forget holidays which can be a great source of stress in a relationship. That is because typically they involve relatives. I feel a lot of couples avoid this topic because there is a level of stress that neither wants to face, but it needs to be addressed as it does not go away. Be proactive as a couple and come up with a plan for the holidays that works for each of you. Understand compromise may be needed, but don't be afraid to tell your relatives that you're forming your own holiday tradition which consists of Christmas in Hawaii. Whatever! You get the point. Discuss your vacation and holiday plans, put it in writing, but give yourselves some flexibility to be spontaneous, which makes life EXCITING!

Personal Space: Respect! Don't tread on each other's personal space. We all need our alone time. Do not touch or go through each other's personal possessions.   We all want our special things left alone, such as: lucky socks, old yo-yos, Girl Scout badges, marble collections, diaries, etc. No one has the right to discard other people's private possession because they find them old or distasteful.

She may want her own hobby room and he may want his man cave, and neither wants you in their respective areas. Just respect each other!

Relatives: This is a true stressor, but I am going to keep it simple because this could be a book in itself. Set boundaries with your relatives! If you are an adult you need to put your relationship above that of your family, because your partner is now your immediate family. No ifs, ands or buts about it. Boundaries include not spending all of your time doing your relatives' bidding. However, discussing the needs of your parents, such as failing health is a necessary part of your relationship. Compromises may have to be considered, but you and your partner need to be honest about this subject. Don't tell your partner what they want to hear, tell them how you feel about the situation. And partners, don't forget that love of relatives should be respected as a part of your loved one's life, thus compassion, generosity and tolerance should be exhibited to all parties concerned.

The Ring: So what do women expect from the men they are dating and loving? A ring of course! That's right put all your individuality away, because here comes the ring. How women wait for the little box with the ring that states you have been picked. Little do they realize that what it really symbolizes is the cycle of life they will be caught up in, and nothing to do about the continuation of love that it is supposed to symbolize. Now I am being a bit tough with you right now, but if you really look at it, you will find that we are sometimes more interested in the ring because of all the "old tradition" it represents, not the truth of the matter--which is, rings do not keep us together - choice does.

This does not mean you can't have proposals or rings. I love jewelry, so I'm all for Contractual Rings. Proposals are great and very exciting for both parties. Of course you can have a "Proposal of Contract", ring and all! It can come from either the man or the woman. But women, if you want to stay with the old tradition of being asked to be part of the unity of a contract, that is perfectly fine. You can still be just as excited when women were traditionally asked to marry and if you want a ring, just let him know. Make sure that you have the ring listed in the contract of whom it remains with if the decision is made to void the contract.

Breach of Contract

We change. We grow. We fall out of love. Whatever the reasons, sometimes we need to break the contract. This process is designed to be complex in the first place in order to have you think about your relationship, so that ultimately you will stay in your partnership longer. However, if you need to be released from your contract, such as in the case of addiction or infidelity, you will need an out.

When you are drawing up your contract, you will need to define the terms of "breach" within the constraints of your contract. You may break it down into major breach of contract which could be one of the consequences of infidelity or addiction. In these cases of breach, the contract would be terminated immediately and the termination clause would take effect.

A minor breach of contract could allow for reconciliation or reconsideration of the contract, before the break-up clause with all distribution of assets and money according to the terms of the contract is triggered.

Freedom to Change

Please don't send me stories of so and so, who is still married and has been in love for 60 years thinking these examples work in favor of marriage. Those folks would have just re-upped for the same amount of time being contracted. Remember, being contracted does not mean you can't spend the rest of your lives together. Being contracted means that you don't have to vow to spending the rest of your life with someone that you most likely will not want to spend the rest of your life with.

Many may feel threatened that he or she won't want to re-up! Look at your own situation and see why you are suffering from those insecurities. Then fix it. Accept it as the human condition that affects us all -- CHANGE!!!!

CHANGE

C -- Conscious

H -- Human

A -- Awareness

N -- Needs

G -- Generational

E -- Evolution

What does this mean? We are conscious human beings. When we look to our consciousness and are aware of ourselves, we will realize that change is inevitable and with that acceptance we evolve in ways that are productive for ourselves and community. Moving with change makes life flow better. If you fight change, it will fight back. For the energy you use to fight it becomes so strong, that in the end, you will find that change wins out. So, you might as well put the emphasis into how you would like to flow with the energy and the change it brings you. Remember, acceptance of change allows a freedom of spirit and energy.

Part Three

Think, Act, Love

Please think before you make any oath, vow or commitment, no matter what it may be, whether it is to bring two people together or with any other act in your life. It is my hope that you will be respectful in all that you do. Love all that there is within this magnificent existence. But be *in love* when it comes to your partner. Do not commit unless you can do so honestly within whatever parameters are put around your relationship.

Be aware--awareness leads us to see others and ourselves in a light that is consciously alert. No fooling ourselves, no putting blinders on, and no lying to ourselves or dismissing our feelings.

Show compassion not only to others but first to yourself. Forgive yourself. We often will forgive others but are so cruel and unforgiving to ourselves!

No matter what and how you may think of a Contract or a marriage, I wish that all of you enjoy the mystery of the "moment" that this earth plane existence can bring you. May you ponder that Love is always in existence and we nurture and bring parts of that infinite Love to each other through our actions of mutual respect, awareness and compassion. Love is not something that is separate from us, it just IS.

Time is not redeemable...it passes so quickly and it is the one thing we cannot get back. We may relinquish what we feel is moral, or of character and integrity, as they can be regained, but not time. Why then, would we waste even one moment in a life that brings us less then the ultimate of all journeys and joy? Live a life filled with as few regrets as possible.

As I still walk this journey in my life, I hope that another "In Love" will come along. One who lights my life with Love, Passion and Respect. In the mean time, I will feel the Love that is Universal and partake of its grandeur. I wish all those who choose a contract to enjoy being in love as they go upon another magnificent voyage. For ALL, I wish you the many experiences of Universal Love.

As Universal Love is infinitely present, we can look to it to touch our lives in many ways. It is the bond that brings us back together as lovers from past lives to this life. It paves the way for new relationships to form for this life and future ones. It is the flame that ignites us so we can rejoice in the union once again.

If you take any one thing away with you from the pages of my little book, may it be that you have the life force within you to experience all of the Universal gifts. Go and use all of your six senses: your eyes to look upon your Loved One, scent to bring the aroma of your Loved One within, to taste all the delights of your Loved One's body, to hear the breath and sounds of your Loved One joined within you, to feel deeply the passion and strength of your Loved One and to allow your intuition to bring you the Loved One of your desires.

Now go and be like wondrous children, with your eyes wide open and love in your heart, bring the passion and desire into you with full abandonment. Ah, to be alive!

Women,
will find their hearts on fire
when he looks within her eyes,
passion takes them jointly,
into the depths of bodies wise.

Men,
will melt with her beauty
she swoons awaiting her fill,
his kisses upon her forehead,
with his hands he holds her still.

Women watch your hearts today,
while his touch brings all that is new
letting the passion take you over,
as he leads you, sends you, brings you to...

Men watch how beauty devours you,
she brings you to your knees,
she demands your kisses to prove your love,
as she leads you, sends you, brings you to...

The moment when your hearts will soar,
with Love that is so divine
lust brings you both to climax,
Oh, bliss in this life of mine.

By Lori Jae

Note from the Author

I refer to myself, as the *Perfect Imperfect Piece of the Perfect Puzzle*

We are all part of the Perfect Puzzle bringing our perfect imperfections together to realize the existence of this earth. It is a part of the ongoing, infinite joy of experience. The infinite universe that holds us, also allows for infinite experience by all. Within this infinite web of existence there are infinite forms and infinite possibilities.

We are vibration and energy and with our very own vibratory being and imprint, we create with our energy. I wish all the marvelous beings on this earth, the creations they desire. Thank you for allowing me to be part of your vibration.

Namaste

All Material Contained in This Book is the Sole Property of Lori Jae

ABOUT THE AUTHOR

Lori Jae currently resides in Scottsdale, AZ and is a mother of two children and proud grandmother of two beautiful boys. She is a psychic channel and medium, a spiritual counselor and a teacher of metaphysics and is sought out for her metaphysical workshops and private intuitive readings. She has been serving in the field for over the last thirty years.

Lori Jae is also an accomplished artist. She is a self-taught acrylic painter that took up painting as a way to work through her Post Traumatic Stress Disorder after a tragic small plane accident of which she survived. Many of her paintings are in private collections around the world and are also housed in several museums.

End Notes:
[i] Magnus Hirschfield Archive for Sexology, History of Marriage in Western Civilization
[ii] Magnus Hirschfield Archive for Sexology, History of Marriage in Western Civilization
[iii] The National Marriage Project at the University of Virginia publishes an annual report titled The State Of Our Unions